BACKYARD ANIMALS

# PRAIRIE DOGS

by Mari Schuh

AMICUS | AMICUS INK

mound

claws

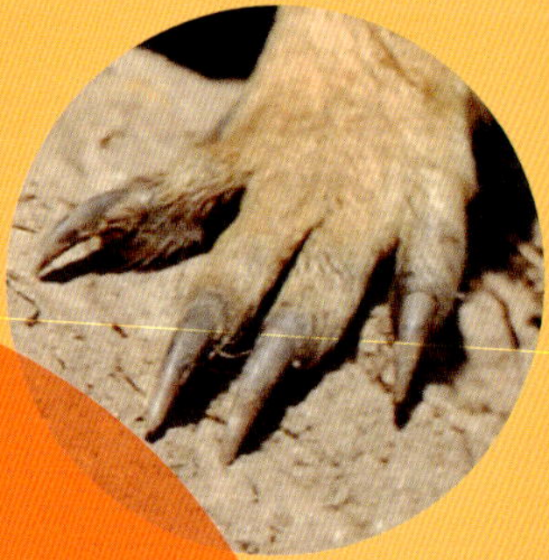

Look for these words and pictures as you read.

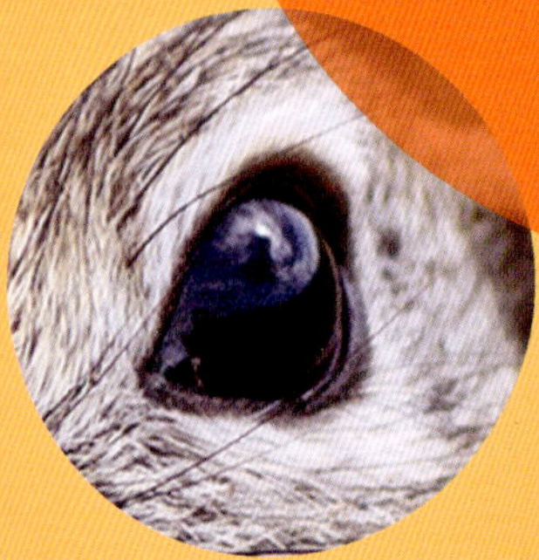

eye

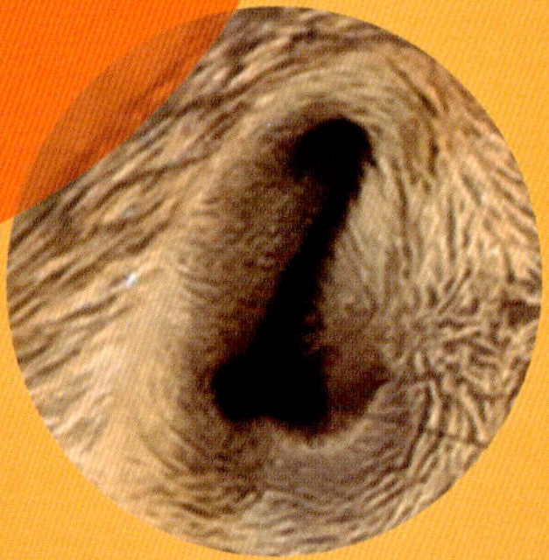

ear

A prairie dog peeks out.
It looks for danger.
Is a coyote near?

Prairie dogs are not dogs.
They are rodents.
They have long front teeth.

Look at the mound.
It leads to a burrow.
It is their home.

**mound**

Look at the claws.
They dig burrows.
A burrow has rooms
and tunnels.

claws

## eye

Look at the eye.
It looks for danger.
It sees a fox far away.

## ear

Look at the ear.
It hears a prairie
dog's call.
The fox is gone.
They are safe.

Later, they hug.
Kiss, kiss!

mound

claws

# Did you find?

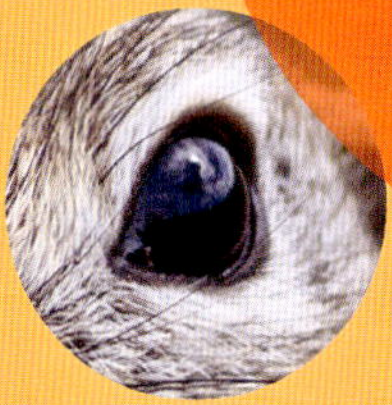

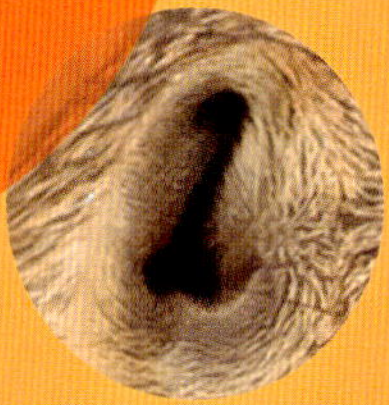

eye

ear

spot

Spot is published by Amicus and Amicus Ink
P.O. Box 1329, Mankato, MN 56002
www.amicuspublishing.us



Library of Congress Cataloging-in-Publication Data
Names: Schuh, Mari C., 1975- author.
Title: Prairie dogs / by Mari Schuh.
Description: Mankato, MN : Amicus/Amicus Ink, [2019] | Series: Spot. Backyard animals | Audience: K to grade 3.
Identifiers: LCCN 2017047792 (print) | LCCN 2017048345 (ebook) | ISBN 9781681515830 (pdf) | ISBN 9781681515458 (library binding) | ISBN 9781681523835 (paperback)
Subjects: LCSH: Prairie dogs–Juvenile literature.
Classification: LCC QL737.R68 (ebook) | LCC QL737.R68 S34865 2019 (print) | DDC 599.36/7–dc23
LC record available at https://lccn.loc.gov/2017047792

Printed in China

HC 10 9 8 7 6 5 4 3 2 1
PB 10 9 8 7 6 5 4 3 2 1

Mary Ellen Klukow, editor
Deb Miner, series designer
Kazuko Collins, book designer
Holly Young, photo researcher

Photos by Age Fotostock 12–13, 14; Alamy 4–5, 8–9; iStock 1, 3, 6–7; Shutterstock cover, 10–11